the ghost at my table

k.h. mari

The Ghost at My Table
By K. H. Mari

Copyright © 2025 by K. H. Mari
SC ISBN: 9781645386605

Cover design by Dana Breunig & K. H. Mari

All Rights Reserved. Written permission must be secured from the publisher to use or reproduce any part of this book, except for brief quotations in critical reviews or articles.

Published by Bubbler Press, an imprint of Orange Hat Publishing
www.orangehatpublishing.com
Wauwatosa, WI

This book is a work of fiction. Names, characters, places and incidents are the product of the author's imagination or are used fictitiously.

The author wishes to emphasize that no "artificial intelligence" or generative text tools were used in the creation of this work. The author and Bubbler Press support human creativity and wish to reassert and maintain its centrality and exclusivity in artistic expression.

to my husband,
for being a love
I never once questioned

autumn somethings

I met you in the fall
When the cold had set into my bones
Thin sheets of ice covered the surface
Of the river and best laid plans

Shrugging off a summer of good intentions
And twenty-something ambitions
I put on my favorite sweater
        and hoped for a little something

we were

A relic of daydreams and simple niceties
Hastened breath and my hands in your jacket
So much for a gentle first-time meeting
First times not so inaugural
      when you see so many familiar glimpses
        behind a new face

November on the shore
Rainbows cast a warm light on your face
I wished to take for myself
Bare my clavicle alongside the mountains I wore
      so you could set it free
           and we could be alone in the dark

I kissed your mouth

    breathed in

        and braced myself

first contact

Contact // One line
Wore this // For you
Something // To prove
Laughter // Your face
HANDS // SWEATER
YOU TOUCH // MY WAIST
Shivers // Midnight
Ecstasy // Awake

chinese food + existential dread

we speak of trust falls
        and noble trysts
        that second night alone
you make a concession
        that makes me lean in
        over steam and rippled cloth
                I can't quite smooth out

your course and mine
        oppose imperative and divine
                I smother each meaning
                until I see what I want
                tracing star paths
                looking for signs
        the value is in its face
                you use the word arbitrary
                enamored with reason
                cards are just cards
                quit trying to read them

still, you look fast
        betwixt what you know
        and what you can concede

you ask for my logic
it's a numbers game, I say
because between gods and people
galaxies spill it all
    with a cup too small
    too trite for one
perception contains multitudes
    for more than just one book
    if I want to believe in anything
    at all
    all it should take is one look
and maybe you like the way that sounds
    or maybe it's the way
        I can convince myself of delusion
        as a man with too many questions
        you've been robbed of the simple
         niceties
        of speculation
    because you take me back home
        take off my clothes
        we don't speak again
        of this little doom
    you take a photo
        of you grabbing my ass
        in a mess of fervor
        I think of a trust fall
            we just maybe are
            orchestrating

it's easy to look forward
    to too far forward at times
    past bedsheets undone discreetly at the
     corners
    I look to your face
        and I see what is now
        and I think no more

does the skin of another
    being seen in oblique beams of light
    faintly guarding the rawest places
    exposing long gone aches and breaks and
     soliloquies
    black and white in theory
        but never at the second glance

        does that erase it all
            just for a moment

tangled thread

My heart is a string
You've effortlessly unraveled
A scarf improperly cast off
I see it there
Coiled around your finger

Is this going to be something—
I think this is going to be something

up and away

When the Midwest is but a patchwork quilt behind glass
Rising through snowdrift clouds
On the front lines against cabin fever
On your way to something greater

When we laugh together on the couch
At that comic who's just a grown-up boy
You quote your favorite bits
And I look at you—
You're the most clever man in the whole world

Do you see the way we eclipse

homeward

I am ever attuned to the way things get caught
Halfway here
Halfway gone
When it's large and consequential and towering
  above me
Would it feel quite so scary if it had a name

You're hours away with hours to go
You ask if you can call me and pass the time

hibernation

I fell in December
        but time and I are so sensitive
I tuck it all under my pillow
        until the feeling of it
        is familiar

First loves are baby birds
So I hunker down for spring
        and we keep each other warm

winter constellations

I remember the crunch of snow
From the aviary sideways stares
We held hands and shared my gloves
And I thanked my lucky stars for the proximity

So much is uncertain that week between Christmas
and New Years

joy

Being the reason you laugh
May be the most treasured thing
I protect it in my arms when I go to bed

We scream the words to that country song in the car
Five minutes unadulterated
How I wish
For the world to cease
So it can bear witness
To the way you look at me
And the way
I memorize it

Melted ice cream and your grin
I kiss the creases around your mouth
      and I see all our ducks in a row on your
        bathroom floor
This love may not burn
      but it is quiet
For a second I think it platinum

the first of its kind

I thought I loved so many before you and who knows
 maybe I did
There was a freshness in my eyes and under my skin
Where wooly bears and starfish made their home
Fresh as a first
      Felt a lot like a last
I crossed my fingers behind my back and hoped for
 the best

what is a man

You're like this and you're like that
And I'm always wringing my hands
A man is an interview
A man is your self-worth
Appease those sorry stares
For showing up alone
A man is a fall I prepare for with a parachute
I turn a man around in my hands
Look for the brightest beam of light

My friends such sweet validation
Spring's first breath of fresh air
Patches sewn onto grass-stained jeans
They said they liked you
And suddenly I'm whole

january affairs

January—
You expose an old wound
And I get you a cake for your birthday
You blow out the candles over and over
As if your age just won't set in
A ritual to call upon fickle Father Time

Joshua Tree—
My mind wanders about the twisted trees
I close my eyes
Visions of deep skies
And I see you standing there
A lantern in your hand
And I think of the way
I'm drawn to the glow

Do you hate an idle weekend like me

valentine's day

I donned your favorite colors
Under my dress
Hoping I could be your favorite too

a cigarette after sex

Taken to the *I love you*
Like a cigarette after sex
A need left wanting
February's everlasting midnights
Leave a lot in the spaces on my back
Between where you placed your lips

The *I think* that came first
Did it soften the blow
For my past versions so burned
By the unrequited

The radio silence
In that dark room
Where I couldn't see the smoke
And how it was rising
My gasping for breath
I think I love you
My cigarette after sex

the yet

Those words are always risky business—
About last night

A prick to my fingertips
Essential for results

You said you weren't there yet
And I said that's okay

I bound my heart together
With whatever I could find
It was still early
And you were still kind

Twiddling my thumbs
Keeping busy

I hung onto the yet for dear life

divine intervention

The devil is in the details
But God is in those first glances

trysts

Years of learning
But animals here under the skin
Subject to our most primal inklings
Not yet swallowed up in fateful gulps
If only we'd done away with each pesky thought
Plucked them out with fingertips
       and little forceps that feel cold to the touch
You take me to your bed
       to your couch
       to your hallway floor
In the night I scream to each and every god
       do they know
       what they have created

lasting effects

Even still you linger—
>Long after my body went cold
>Fingertips tracing over those places
>Where I had so much to hide
>Where your mouth had left fleeting marks
>And your breath had ignited in me
>An ethereal glow all your own

My skin is a pool—
>Consecutive halos as you breach the surface
>And tangle up my heartstrings
>I think I hear a melody
>Building to precisely the sound
>I've been waiting for all along

I feel it once more as it nears crescendo—

thoughtful recognition

I think I can see it sometimes—
A lightness in your eyes—
> They're feathers on still water
> Crescent curves from tip to tip
> A convergence of nature and art
>> I only scarcely dream of

It's your careful embrace—
> A kiss on the cheek
> Something so fragile I speak at a whisper
> For fear I may scare it away entirely

So I bow my head—
> And study how you've interlaced our fingers

I'm quite adjusted—
> To the absence of words
> So I read the writing on the walls
>> and keep my suspicions to myself

singapore fortune

Palm reader of seventeen months past—

Back when I believed anything—
> so long as there was a little inkling of hope
> for me
> for something
> for anything greater than twenty-two years
> know
> and how much is that really

A finger along the creases—
> a canyon
> dried rivers
> the veins of a maple leaf
> broken English and that smell
> how I can't erase durian

—Did you really foretell

aeronautics

I used to watch the airplanes
Make their streams in the blue

I folded paper to put on your desk
Talked shit about childhood shittalkers
Let you take me to bed
       and I would grab your hair
       and you would tell me the same joke twice

We shared your twin bed
And we'd sleep with our backs touching
       We tried so hard for anything else
You taught me how to fly
I took so many notes
       and I fell
              and I fell
                     and I fell

I watch the airplanes
And somehow, they've changed

spring

I dreamed of your family's tennis courts in fall
And the bluffs over the lake where we stopped to breathe
I met your friends and you met mine

My clothes in your bedroom
A toothbrush by the sink
Small favors
A little sprout peeking out sidewalk cracks
On my knees I watched it grow

eclipses

A fascination fit for letters and lists
A man a vista a mountain-view terrace
We singularly lusted for greater longitudes
An eclipse of taste

I thought myself good and fit company
Erected a shrine to your crooked kisses
      and the way you poked fun
A permanent marker underlined
      the way I say February
And took tallies
      of how many times I parked wrong

I thought these the signs
      of a gracious epoch

sunday dreaming

My cup emptied out into the universe
Droplets scattered amongst the stars
All the way down
Our fingers traced
To that rocking chair that remembers
Gentle whispers of a house and kids
I wanted that hope in your eyes forever

gods

I prayed to gods that haunted
the gaps between my fingers
and the hollow spaces under my ribs
where my ghosts liked to light signal flares

asked them why I was built this way
made of soft clay
from the basins where rivers once thrived
place a droplet on my tongue

bare

I stripped myself down for you and I stood in shame
as I peeled off layer after layer, pleading for you to
find something that you like as I caught one corner of
my fingertip and pulled slowly up my arm and across
my shoulders and down until all but my desire to
please was scattered about the floor.

false beliefs

Devout to the entertainment
I thought that bet safe once

Treason in the background
Disguised   misshapen   twitterpated
A figure I've drawn once   twice   thrice
Cross my Ts
Cross my eyes
A compliment for you
A pilgrimage for me

A sermon's most moral subject
I build your pyres and drink your wine
Tunnel vision   vague descriptions
Seek my puzzle piece narrative

Please rise
Body   blood   trick of the light
Passages gleaming and my mind deceiving
The shine of something more
It whispers
Westwestwestwestwest

What are the downs
My gaze so fixed
A horizon of striated glass

Devout to the entertainment
I worship on my knees

when you wanted to go

The words that changed everything
Punctuated by silence
If you could possibly see
The way I was plummeting
If you could possibly see
Panic's desperate hands
Clawing at my throat

Would this have changed
Anything at all

I didn't want to know the ending
So I never asked
But this was a conclusion
With plenty of foreshadowing

And we pretended
We didn't know

continental divides

Oh mountain air
Oh mountain vistas
They pulled us together
Then just as easily
May just tear us apart

How could something I loved so
Be so wretched with my heart

just a quarter to play

The scale tips
Heavy with the weight of my grievances
The excuses jingling in my pocket

I should have been a welcome imposition
Instead with each week—
        You and new views
        Me and new propositions

I slip a coin into the slot
Because the horse is worn
Where I put my hands
And I have the change for some predictability

no coming around

Pale ale straight from Midas
You swear I'll come around to it—
      around Georgian mountain paths
      and men who look like you
We tromp in the mud, and I bleach my clothes white

My coin purse is empty
But I pretend the lint is currency—
      urgency in my bones
      a splinter under my fingernail
My hands no good with buttons

Gold gives birth to gray

a sinking suspicion

I   get this   feeling

I   might be
           loving you
                        all

                                  wrong.

changing seasons

All of me changed
Summer to fall to winter
That full moon crashed
Into you and me to us and we

I laid awake with you
Resisting metamorphosis

royalty to me

This crown
I had so dutifully made
I adorned your head
I cut my hand
When I placed it askew
But you just looked so handsome
Pursed my lips
Bit my tongue
I let them in—
Some more mistakes

dirty laundry

I took off my clothes
And then yours too
Doubts disguised in a messy little pile

So many things to put to bed

letting your guard down

Sweetness in your eyes
A drink in your hand
Rationale impeded

You held me so tight
A raft out to sea

seamstress

I was a springtime bird
I could use anything to build
Take any kind word and soft look
And turn it to thread

I was an antique doll
A needle in my hand
Mending all my rips and tears
A vague reconstruction

politeness + power

You know what they say about politeness and power
Mine wrapped with a bow
All that remained were the crumbs I picked up with
 my fingertips
I chastised the way my insides begged for more

Your indifference and my proclivity to self-sabotage
A match made in heaven
Hell is bent all out of shape
It looks a lot like my paranoia

high altitudes

Frigid mountain peaks are less treacherous—
    when the silence is interrupted
A blizzard in your eyes—
    it surrounds and surrounds and surrounds
Bluster to me—
    what could you see through the whiteout
I cling to you for warmth

skyscrapers

There are days I take refuge in myself
When there are no words left
When language leaves such a gaping hole
I clutch the phone with shaking fingers
       and you say nothing
Because feelings are bigger than both of us
And to look them in the face
One must turn his chin directly skyward
       and hope that he likes what he sees

If these feelings are not a sight to behold
Then
What can we do but hide under cover

carnival games

aching desperation
it's all just a chase
pursuit of wit and more than a sideways glance
—do they even know your name
memorialized
a photo on the wall
when wheat field sunlight catches it indiscriminately
a smile a nod goddamn just something please
something your mother would have looked at with
 ease
but that's quite the problem isn't it
i don't have the source material
but the words are on your face
bring you down lift you up
it's just a fucking carnival ride
i bring you a pretzel and the trinkets i won
it's all just a big disgrace

space

You said you needed space to think things through, and I thought that this was it. There was a day of silence between us, the first one, the only one, and my awareness of it was so pointed and acute that maybe it should have been it, but a day later it was the same old story, and I wore your shirt and things were quiet.

authentic pretenses

When you think of where you could be
Do you forget your hand grasping my thigh
The way it sends me
The way it makes me want to kiss your neck
And leave a mark for you to carry with you
So I will be more
Than a rearview low tide
That you soon enough forget

Dreams of here
Dreams of there

I breathe in my most authentic pretenses
And all is well

gas leak

Copious nights overflowing into days
There is a ringing in my ears
Best left uninvestigated

I overanalyze every tiny tragedy of faith in you
But gone unseen behind my eyes there is no harm in
 a little mania
So I gaslight myself till I'm high on the fumes
        and spirits dance around the room

1950s daydream

New clothes
Newfound recipes
Donna Reed would be so proud
From where she stands
In the corner of my mind
I smell fresh bread and Pine-Sol
And wonder whose idea it all was

Time is money
Money is proof
I can rhyme and reason a whole lifetime
With a good excuse

card games

You enamored me
King of hearts
                I dug so deep
                Queen of spades

"at least i'm someone's"

merciless honesty
cruel comedy
maybe you didn't think twice about it
but i thought a thousand times

did vulnerability shake your ground
send you searching for something stable to cling to
it left some inner sadness in plain sight
an unexplored bruise exposed
you smeared its color from you to me

i am no shakespeare
not profound
       —merely sincere

why did it hurt when i said
you're my best friend

gentle persuasion

How could I believe myself so persuasive
I could change entire trajectories and grand schemes
  and master plans
They predated me
Stretched in every direction when I sought out
  horizons
        with new colors and unfamiliar shapes
Melancholic sounds break free from my grasp
        even though I'd held them with all my might

I am an artisan of the pedantic
Painting with my tiny brushes
        and dipping into my thimble of water
I'm so entirely encapsulated
I don't notice when a bluebird flaps its wings in the
  Rockies
        and blows the whole house down

springtime rain

I am a master of the subtle art
Of breaking myself down
Check the ticket
Compare my driver's license photo
Pat myself down
Looking for bombs

They were hidden at one time so well
I keep them all
In boxes in my basement
But April is the same with every year
A little water
Makes cardboard so weak

morning tides

I thought it was love
But maybe it was force
Foaming along the coast after a storm
Pockets full of pebbles
Worn smooth
Daybreak pulls me apart
Puts me back together

What is meant to be waits for its cue

twisted trees

You grasp the top of the door
Lingering here over me—
Look.
I see it now—
I see it clear
Each and every layer

Of what is frozen and what has turned to vapors
If I could give you the keys—
Drive.
Would it set—
Would it evolve
Where would we be

A hotel room outside of Palm Springs
Taking Polaroids of Joshua Trees—
Freeze.
Take me with—
Take the keys
Please fucking take the keys

don't close your eyes

Love and grief grow hand in hand
        from time to time
One perhaps quieter
        than the other
Tiptoeing around the truth
        and peering around corners
Whispering bitter somethings
        when your eyes are closed

breathing in the fumes

I begged—
With my eyes
With fresh-picked flowers
With dinner for two
With clothes on the floor
And my best behavior
All the things I would have given freely
Loaded now
Marked with an asterisk
Tainted with a silent plea

You resisted—
With averted eyes
With abrasive honesty
With curiosity curtailed
With no thoughts of me
And telling me that to my face
All this to put some distance between us
Pushing shoving
Tolerating everything
To keep it from being harder than it has to be

I wondered—

With bated breath
With midnight crises
With my fortress crumbling
With an inkwell mind
And under-eyes like bruises
What are these smoke signals I read
Are they real at all
A mind's trick
Thin ice mirage
What if the crisis is inside me

I caved—
What is that
What does it mean
Why does my mind collapse so
Oh house of mirrors
Where is the proof
What if I am the madness
What if I am the doom
Ripples wrinkles smoothsmoothsmooth
Smile and smile and smile and smile and

rocky mountain illusions

I wish I was born a mountain
Unruffled by the coyote's laughter

oaths + treatises

We hear those voices
A crackle in my lungs
The writing so embedded
Within the marrow
Incantations running a thin line
Down those spinal ridges
Where one can simply pretend
They need another to read them
Another to trace with delicate fingertips
Those tricky scars
That look like words and promises
To tell a lie
When I was there all along

Seasons like to flicker
From deities who murmur with harsh breath
To make the pendulum swing
Do they believe
The way my compendium of reasons
Is taken by the gales
They are doing good by me
Desperate tales and desperate fibs
Beckon the first tulips on

Sacred truths bite at my feet
Bated breath makeshift star signs
They set the constellations alight
But even dead stars still shine

We broke bread
Centuries past would call that an oath
Something in deep that won't come clean
Gentle words gentle mistakes
The hurt inside flashes a devilish grin
A twist of legs
Hardwired so reckless
Tore down the curtains before the moon arose
The court made its choice
Spitfire and aloed burns
Trust the process it's just slight madness
I curse the harlequin in the mirror
She chants *proof proof proof*

young love

Is this what love is supposed to be—
    Moments of bleak nothing
    A view of an untouched landscape of snow
    Deprived of landmarks and the voices
        that take tallies
        and leave smoke signals frozen in air
    Of creeping ivy overtaking the lattice
    Beautiful in an understated kind of way
    Penetrating in secret stone I once believed
     solid
—at twenty-three

homemade ghost

I throw a sheet over my head
Beg you to see me
Scissors and jagged eyes

Summertime girl
Scarcely beheld in true light

kitchen views

You were making plans
I was making dinner
I watched the timer
You watched the game

I would have been everything—
You didn't have to ask
You would have done anything—
I never thought to ask

unsavory

Looks like you've had your fill of me
You've cleared your plate to your heart's content
You push the rest aside to be taken away
Tell me the moment I became so unsavory

glass faces

I thought I was walking on eggshells
    when I was treading
    on the porcelain remains of myself
And what a similar sound
They make under my feet

exposure

I was breathless
Blustering snow was stripping me down
Lips parted
And suddenly I was alone with you when you stopped
  to talk
Gasoline a ripe fragment of reality I could almost
  grasp

And where I should have made a desperate appeal—
Put a stake through us—
Anything to break the monotony that was killing me
  slowly
There was radio silence

Teardrops crystallized
You looked at me from the driver's seat
As the glass separated us still
Why wouldn't you let me in

implications

Maybe you suddenly said you didn't like holding hands
Because it kept you from leaving

Maybe I was hurt by that
Because that was the last thing I wanted

contagious

Does the brokenness you perceive in yourself—
  Cracks on the wall
  Your fingertips to mine
  Touches a commodity once
  An oddity now
—Do you think they taint me

knotted

The words get lost under my pulse
    Too afraid to come to my own defense
    Too afraid to pull the plug
I am suffocated
    When all I have to do
    is loosen my grip

artwork

Make the best of the silence
Keep me company with your persuasion
Take off your coat and your reasons too
I think we can both see
I'm determined with my misery
Take your colors and I'll take mine
You paint a mural
I paint an autumn green

inner calamities

The track record haunts me in the aftermath
Of what could have been
Fight flight freezefreezefreezefreezefreeze
Robbed of nerves
Wealth of inhibitions
That loosen belts
And tighten lips
The key in my pocket
I snap it off in the lock

I kept all the receipts
The angle to reach my heart
Is no more familiar to anyone but me
That voice that I'm not sure knows better
It tells me to bolt from the weaponry
But fast is this broken glass lodged
The words are here
Stuck amongst my clavicles
But am I worth the trouble
The qualms may just swallow me up
In one unlucky high tide

This could be history in the making

But little trivial things
Have a trickle-down effect
Tremors are earthquakes
To the most delicate places

Trip the wire
Ransacked landscapes
I peer over the edge and fear the bottom

Nights take their time
Agonizing lonesome bodies in bedsheets
Who make light of the way their soul is dying
I want to promise it will be worth the wait
To speak unutterable things that may tear this place
 asunder
If patience and time are best left uncounted
On my most uncertain days

Wildfires everywhere
On my clothes they catch
I know the sound of the alarms I should pull
In the lick of the flames, I see a familiar face
I trade my gloves for matches

I flinch
I do not know which promises to trust

Will you be here when dawn breaks

more

I.
You are not where I am
Sometimes it hurts
And sometimes it gets the best of me
Slow songs out the speakers pulling from deep in my soul
      rivers in which I could drift away if I didn't
        want to fight any longer
But fight I do
      and fight I will
And maybe it will be the death of me
      but what if it is the life of me

II.
I could have left
Everyone has been telling me to leave
And though they may know
They do not feel
      and that is the whole disjuncture—
Between them and me
      between you and I

III.
I love you just the way you are
I say
Even though you look upon yourself a damaged mass
        and me with guilt
Wishing there could be more

antigravity

There is no falling
Beyond the atmosphere
Lingering amongst the dogwoods
I study the galaxies
And wonder
Even still
Up there
Did you fall maybe a little

just another sorry trinket i guess

I gave you my heart—
And you left it there on the dining room table
It's where you put all the things you don't have
      ample
              space
                      for
A vacuum for the miscellaneous
A catch-all for all the sorry trinkets

We ate dinner on the couch

I gave you my heart—
      I watched it gather dust

skin exposed

Each curve a moment to take me deeper
The days blurring—
      warmer and longer
      begging
      take off your jacket
      hibernation breaking
My legs are bare now this time of year
But still heaviness lingers in my bones
      I can't seem to pull it out
      I can't seem to put my finger on it
          or maybe I won't
            or maybe I simply cannot bend that
              direction

That song keeps coming on
Instinct changes it every time
      The heaviness grows so weighty
      It rises to my skin where I get too clear a view
          and I can't look at it
          I won't look at it

Summertime melancholia
I let the song play

    Once
            Only once
Curiosity and a hunger to feel
And I know now why it cuts me so cleanly

Fortune teller
Fate maker
Palm reader
    It can see my face
        and it knows

redeeming words

The words I heard burned me
But they weren't the words I was waiting for

The things I saw rebuffed me
But shapes can be deceiving in the glow of the gaslight

So I listened to your stories
Awaiting my cue

But there was no story you could tell me
They weren't meant to save me

ill-fated imagery

I.
I am paper thin
Somehow I can always feel it in my wrists
Yet my reflection feels as large as can be
        filled up on melatonin and self-loathing
Purple crescent moons balance on my cheekbones
I run a mile to make them glow
        and change the tides

II.
It flashes back to you
Calling yourself broken
And talking about the girl
        you fell in love with before
I throw up trying to picture her face

ground zero

Ground zero needs something more
A couple words
To begin and to end
The bombs that we lay

a fragile thing

Am I naive to believe
After all these days
I can still trust you
To be delicate

day into night drinking

I.
My friend cried tequila tears
You asked if you were the problem

II.
Then you kissed me in the basement
Like you really fucking meant it
I saw stars amidst cobwebs and rusted paint cans

III.
You told me I looked nice
When we slept on the floor
And I wondered where all this had been

IV.
Was it drunken honesty
Or drunken embellishment

V.
When the sun descended
And the bottles all but retained a bite to my nose
Can you please tell me—
Who was I

thirteen

We called it
I pushed and told you to decide
I hated the idleness the limbo
The purple cardigan I wore—
I thought about what I almost wore instead

Somehow the intrusive thoughts crescendo at pivotal moments

There's something so unlucky about the thirteenth
But maybe some unspoken goodness as well

nail in the coffin

One last kiss goodbye
All I felt was shame
What an embarrassment
What a laughingstock
Cursing at blackbirds building nests and staking claims
Despairing over a man who was surprised he cried at all
You should be sad
You should be fucking sad

this mess of me

Look at the mess I've made
Thread and needles scattered on the floor
The scale tells me a dozen pounds of who I once was
Have gone
I poke and prod and can't seem to see where
But so much is perspective and so much less is reality
And all I can see beyond the melancholia
Is how deep I get under my own skin

I tell you how it hurts
On the bathroom floor dry-heaving all my best
　intentions
Why is porcelain always so cold

transparent

I was spread so thin, I watched with bitter fascination the way light passed through my hands, illuminating the shapes of everything they held inside. Everything that held them together, made them function, was suddenly clear to me, and I wanted to chop them off at the wrists.

from the back of the wardrobe

I cannot help but imagine
A wayward procession of skeletons
At home in the recesses of the wardrobe
Untangled themselves from the hangers and coats
Caught up to me—
    teetering
        consistent
            strength in numbers
Grabbed ahold and tightened my lips—
    hushed my voice
        until I spoke
            words of obedience

the jester never lies

I chose the misery
Over the lonely
Despite the jester in the mirror
Wailing and taunting
Honey, don't deceive yourself
You were lonely then too

even dust glimmers in the light

i see it all like rhinestones in air
and i think it silver and gold

boys who only called at night
and boys who called those threats a compliment

they really set a standard
i set me up for failure

firstfruits

What's left of the firstfruits
Have all gone to waste
I should have done away with them
Once they gave way under my touch

evicted

I deserted my integrity
Took the keys
The last change from pride's pockets
By the time I'd returned home
The air was cold
Grass flourished in the walkway cracks
And the locks were changed

    —and for what?

played a stupid game

Promising me
You'll always be
Rooting for me
A consolation prize
Marks for participation

Well wishes
Seldom erase
The way it hurt
When I wished for so little

sea creature

Brittle—
Long hours in the hammock
Caught in unfamiliar tides
Floating lantern glow
Looking but never seeing
I am a sand dollar

phantom things

I would have been
Your first mate
Your last mate
Your housemate for a season

I stand here and I whisper
At a wisp of smoke
I could have sworn was you
I would have spent
Days and days
Chasing those ghosts
Touching those apparitions

I really wish it could have been you

schematics

Something better off left disengaged
Was it because of you or was it because of me

Untrained eyes look for the one to blame
Talk their talk of disrespect

Draw lines
Take sides

They just don't know
We built this bomb together

kindling

I'm not addicted to the drama
Of keeping quiet
Always suspicious
Making all these assumptions
I just don't have the gumption
To break the pattern
It's my family tree
The roots run deep
All this goddamn generational trauma
It's in the mirror
It's under the rug
We fucked on in our winter coats
It's on the tip of my tongue
I'd climb the ladder but I just can't reach the next rung
I guess we'll just pass it by
When I count the streetlights
And buy you beer
And write you a note
Why couldn't you do better
What were you so scared of
At least it knows for me
It all goes back in time

I smell the fuel
Light the match
And I wonder why
Why does it all burn around me

one shallow grave

Indiscretions outnumber all my reasons
For burying myself under six feet
Of all those little needles
Hoping to make that grave feel a little more shallow

What is it I have done
I took my intentions, and I used them
That juvenile training in nicety and standing so still
I abused them
I crossed blades and lines
Left myself so many warning signs

I kept myself behind glass for you
Or was it for me—
It was all the wrong season
Hot and cold—
Rain and snow—
I lent you my coat and my scarf
And my goddamn skin and bones and said
Why, what a wonderful day!

The tornado siren so faint
I'd have known if I'd just looked up
Broken glass
Broken glass

collapse

If only change could be spontaneous
Rather than a chain reaction
A turnkey recoil from the hurt
Backing away
        from the fire
        from the sirens
                and the angles of your face
                dyed blue and red
Before it all collapsed

Sometimes when a building
        comes down upon you
It is not the weight that kills you
It is the dust

queen of nothings

I.
I tore the whole temple asunder
Ripped the purple tapestries
Took my scepter to the stained glass
Sat upon my throne all alone

II.
Why oh why
Were the lights so dim
The staff all resigned—
I heard in the courtyard
I'm the butt of the joke

III.
And I screamed and I screamed and I screamed

glacial currents

Glacial rivers
Down down down they chase
Knowing their course
Carving the stones to their will
Cold to the touch
Ancient waters
Fighting time
Is to push against them
Against sense and reason
To wade upward
To taste shivering handfuls
To let the drops fall from your chin
And tell them they are all wrong

The fish play with sensibility
Up up up they climb
Waiting eyes take their time
Thirsting for gravity defiers
Spent on unseeable feats
Illogical trysts
Jaws agape just above the surface

Little prey, little prey

How could you not have known

dog bites

I say that I'm fine
But I'm always there in my mind
It's the old cliché
Let that dog lie
On that entryway rug
In your sheets
But now it bares its teeth to me

I'd never loved anyone else before
I guess I just didn't know how to do it

one man's crossing

I.
Sometimes
I can trick
The light in my eyes
Into believing this is all unremarkable

The human proclivity
To hang tight to the woe
When my hands are full
Maybe these misfit days
Can teach me
To choose what I carry

II.
Sometimes
I feel like
I am moments away
From turning back to clay

How can I bloom where I am planted
When I cannot
Call the loam by its name
Without looking up

Fingers dyed red

III.
Sometimes
Dawn's perfect breaking
Feels a lot like tragedy
After cursed nights of spinning

When the pines whisper
Do they fear to raise their voice
Does the harvest moon
Tell the wheat to tremble
This twisted altar beneath my ribs
A god so mortal in this light

IV.
Sometimes
One breath held
High tides remind me
The sharpest glass can grow smooth

Time will mouth its spells
Same old introspective incantations
That foresee me becoming
Something far less tragic
Than a bridge that collapses
Over one man's crossing

Let that current go

mn

You asked me to Minneapolis
Back when it was all still new
I go there a lot now
Without a first or second thought

Thank God you never took me
What's worse than the broken plans
Is the unseeing—
It takes so much balance
To turn a memory on its head

entangled

Shame on me—
>Caught on all those little details
>I could only see under the microscope
>In the middle of the night
>Under the covers with a flashlight
>Charting your trajectory
>With a map and a permanent marker
>Waiting for the pivot

Shame on you—
>Your course was set
>A ruler-straight line
>You knew there was no curve
>And I was in your orbit
>We were two knotted threads
>For you to set parallel
>And you did nothing

fool's errand

My blunt instruments
Could not change you

Oh lord
How you changed me

self-sabotage

Good intentions a sorry balm for the pain
You were hurting me
        I let you do it
You didn't know
        I knew better
Lessons I pretended to have never learned
        If only to keep you
One never suspects betrayal
From someone who looks so complicit

maneuvering

He didn't mean it
Accidents are so easy to explain away
Motives buried under earth's crust
While you look for views
And I look for clovers
With enough leaves to matter

These intentions shoot to kill
I wish I would have ducked

mantra one

LOVE SHOULDN'T TAKE CONVINCING
LOVE SHOULDN'T TAKE CONVINCING
LOVE SHOULDN'T TAKE CONVINCING
LOVE SHOULDN'T TAKE CONVINCING
LOVE SHOULDN'T TAKE CONVINCING
LOVE SHOULDN'T TAKE CONVINCING
LOVE SHOULDN'T TAKE CONVINCING
LOVE SHOULDN'T TAKE CONVINCING
LOVE SHOULDN'T TAKE CONVINCING
LOVE SHOULDN'T TAKE CONVINCING
LOVE SHOULDN'T TAKE CONVINCING
LOVE SHOULDN'T TAKE CONVINCING
LOVE SHOULDN'T TAKE CONVINCING

pointed truths

You never lied
But what did you call
Those secrets that you kept

You took a pin
To my overinflated sense
Of what this was

You twisted the knife
Talking of all those dreams
That never included me

stocks

did you pull your investment
when an insider told you
we were going to crash
leaving me
to
  n
   o
    s
     e
      d
       i
        v
         e

crevices

I've been keeping
Something just so wicked
Here behind my eyes
Discussing and dismissing
Call you out
Drop you down
From my lips
These words they twist
Ivy vines and sacred times
Run these tests
Hold my tongue
Just as long as I can
Can you fill this space
My feet kick rocks down
Stopwatch buttons
Brand new eyeliner
I turn out the lights and

petty inclinations

Sometimes
I imagine
A drunken call I could make
Come clean with all the grievances
My shoulders are sore from carrying
It comes in waves
These bursts of resent
And I think
Of how I could just let
The undertow push those words
A little thirty proof tempts
A little tit for tat

Sometimes
I imagine
Ruining your day
So you'll finally know how it felt
When you would ruin all of mine

hindsight

Do you ever wonder
If you left a wound
Do you see my pictures
And think I forgot

My relentless optimism
And the way you looked at me
The truth is
Imagining it now
A taste so bitter
I want to spit it out
I wish I could let it
Disappear with the winds
Pinch it out
A candle burned all the way down

Sometimes I tell myself
It would have been better
If you hadn't been so kind
A quicker conclusion
To the ending I dragged out

tolerations

I turn a mirror onto this blame
It feels like such a crime
It feels like such a shame
To feel this tolerated

You wanted red
When I lived in utter blue
But I changed it all
I fucking changed for you

mantra two

LOSING ME SHOULD BREAK YOUR HEART
LOSING ME SHOULD BREAK YOUR HEART
LOSING ME SHOULD BREAK YOUR HEART
LOSING ME SHOULD BREAK YOUR HEART
LOSING ME SHOULD BREAK YOUR HEART
LOSING ME SHOULD BREAK YOUR HEART
LOSING ME SHOULD BREAK YOUR HEART
LOSING ME SHOULD BREAK YOUR HEART
LOSING ME SHOULD BREAK YOUR HEART
LOSING ME SHOULD BREAK YOUR HEART
LOSING ME SHOULD BREAK YOUR HEART
LOSING ME SHOULD BREAK YOUR HEART
LOSING ME SHOULD BREAK YOUR HEART

all but one

i cannot trust my midnight thoughts
i miss yous cut in
forgetting how back then i would miss me

i
feel
so
much

i count them out on my fingers
knowing every name
but i look them in the eyes and i know

regret
is
not
one

post mortem

This love has made me into a gravedigger
Who never lets that dirt settle

Wide awake full moon nights
Convinced the body has changed
Each plunge of the shovel
Each creak of hinges
Multiplies the rot

Nature beckons me
With snow and ice
To leave it to rest
But madness
Cannot be coaxed
Except by defeat

a double-edged love

Did you take antiseptic to the wounds I created
Cleansed everything that I touched
Were my letters a little insult to injury
A master of self-preservation
Angel of my dreams or just a man

I grieve it now
Like a death
Sometimes I forget
It was your loss too

nurture fights dirty

self-defense is an art
that requires so little thought
how did i take it
and pull it apart in my hands

i defied nature for you—

why was my first instinct
something that hurt me so
a death wish
a conquest
a ruse of a game

why was there something so natural
in taking myself apart
piece
      by
            p i e c e

# of gentleness + passion

Back in those days
I wrote a list
Of all the things
I loved about you
Once a love unscathed
Now in that bed of ash
Never once did I think
Of a list for me
And maybe that is why
There is nothing left standing

There is so much glory
In self-denial
Love as a lion
Wrought quiet sacrifice as a lamb
I fear the beast has swallowed me whole
If only I had known
What this something was going to be
It scarcely feels like glory at all

chronic aches

The healing overtakes the whole affair
In magnitude and longevity
I will be the first to admit
We were not a ferocious love
But this bygone tryst
Is taking its time
Leaving my bones

the ghost at my table

Credit now
Where credit is due
This calls for a toast
For all of this—
The ghost at my table
Idle haunting
Unfinished business
So long ago
I opened that door
Now lessons learned
Priorities sorted
But why in that chair
Does it remain

The clock strikes twelve
I make it some tea
We'll waste away the night again
Deeds and deep words
They change it none
By now
Lady Luck and Father Time
Must have turned a blind eye
I cannot remember now

Which came first—
The overstaying of its welcome
Or when I fixed it a plate

Some days I pass it by
Nearly forget it entirely
This haunt can sit so still

In twilight's crux out my window
Neither and both
Day and night—
Everything comes out blue
I get caught by its shape
That look of knowing
We have each other memorized now
Is it a comfort—
This half being alone
Neither here nor there
A preoccupation of thens and nows
That take up enough space
All else I put on a high shelf
Beside the smelling salts and blueprints
That once had greater plans

How do you expel
Something so entwined
Where do I end
Where does my ghost begin
Has what is ours ever truly been mine

just deserts

When did you stop
Being a wound to heal
And start being
A blunt object
I punish myself with

What did I do
To deserve it

because of me

Judas, Judas
Next of kin
The best betrayal
This victimless sin
—I've saved it just for Me

Chain link fences
Ill-timed escape
My bridge has burned
Into a familiar shape
—Why does it look like Me

Why am I trapped
In here with Me
Gnaw through the bone
If it means I'm free
—No one hates quite like Me

Insincere or insecure
Depends on the season
Liar, liar, I say to Me
Loneliness is the only reason
—Deception looks no good on Me

Sisyphus begged
If only I had learned
Quicker now quicker still
A futile man once secerned
—An apology I owe to Me

turning point

Last night I had a dream
That you'd moved on
Posting about a girl on your Instagram

Every other night
We fooled around
With that idea of each other

This time
I saw you with her
And I frowned
And I said
I would have been so miserable

looking backward

Your town doesn't get a rise in me any longer
Those thoughts no longer hot to the touch
Caught under the summer rays
Now under a blanket of snow

Where you used to live doesn't stir my heart
When I go there to dance
Once sharp on my fingertips now worn smooth
I nearly forget what it all felt like

you were just a man

You were just a man
Not a code to be cracked
Sweet reward in hiding
Seeking safety in our combination
How I spun in the nights
Listening for the click

You were just a man
Not an idol to worship
Whose wine I spilled
Your stories were not parables
I searched for salvation
In all the wrong places

You were just a man
Not my one true love
A vision once so clear
Is clearer still in a way so contrary
When love is lost
A journey is charted

You were just a man
Not someone to be persuaded

Now just a stranger
I keep in my furthest peripherals
I get it now
The lessons of it all

simplicity

one day
i hope
to make peace
with how complicated
we all are

i think then
it will make grace
so simple

inner voices

Maybe the root of this
Is that voice in me that knows

The voice predicts every path
Before it is taken

The voice that knows me
And tells me

You are worthy of the love
You so desperately sought after

i'm sorry (part one)

Best foot forward
Perfect first impression
I suppose I talked a real good game
Kissing you in the dark
I fall so quickly most times
But never so deep as then
Our dreams were parallel lines
And that made me think forever

I did so much
Purely on assumption
Because I was so afraid to ask
I thought heaven with you
Was a fair trade
So I was in hell in private
My fears felt close to detonating
And saying so would light the fuse

I put you in jail
For not being forward
When I was championing the role
On your couch
Sick to my stomach

Deciding neither of us
Possibly deserved better
I was ready to be everything you wanted
At the cost of being everything I needed

It was love I swear it was
Minus the know-how
And transparency
And I chose you and I chose you
With reckless abandon
Because once I had heard
That love is a choice
And all it would take for you
Was a little persuasion

But you never lied to me
The way I lied to myself
Spoonfed delusions
Of a true love's transformation
Rewards for nerve and naivety
Chalk it up to a pretense
That I did you a favor
From a pariah to a prince
That if I'd been just a little more perfect
Then maybe you would have believed it

All these things
I've left unsaid
And that's my cross to bear

Closure is a tricky thing
My mind loves to leave me hanging
On the precipice of what if
Can you feel the way
I have lingered
Haunted and haunting
Turning this around and around
Memorizing this time capsule
Until you have ceased to be a mystery
And become only a memory
Of fondness and lessons learned
I hope soon
I can leave you in peace

i'm sorry (part two)

I am bold
Until I get what I want
I speak volumes
Then tear out every page
Afraid of the conflict
The climax
An ounce of dismay

Perfection is betrayal
Of one's most defining phases
We do not chastise the moon
Nights lacking perfect glow
For these nights
Are most common
And who am I
If not common

I am but
An assemblage of parts
Oh what nerve I have
To pretend
Such parts are unneeding
Such parts are not failing

Why is it
I felt so undeserving
Of such care
Too afraid of losing someone
To realize I'd already deserted myself

I am the product
Of dust
Trapped under the rug
And for the first time
Exposed to the light
I can breathe clean

There is so much trust
To be re-earned
I flinch each time I feel
For I see the love in excess
Extended beyond my fingertips
And realize
I must keep some for myself

This fear of unbecoming
Perhaps has kept me
From becoming
Anything at all
When I could have
Given myself the chance
To be everything

summer love letter

I.
Whenever did the bitterness set sail
The horizon an idyllic display
A love note's envelope in a bottle
Pink and blue and golden
When I hold it up to the light
I see the outlines of thoughtful words

—I wrote in cursive back then

II.
Daylight and amiable calls and sweet sangria
The taste of a season I hate to miss
I fall in love each and every time
As the trees turn green and back again to red
And the ghosts in the mirror turn kind again

—Precious are the days I like what I see

mountain dreams

I heard you bought a house in the Front Range
Planted some roots in that wandering soul
Once always so on the move
      —Remember when that was my dream too?

I imagine long halls
Your photographs collaged on the walls
Nooks and crannies where you feel at home
As much as Colorado's wide open spaces
      —I hope you've given yourself the best

Are you a little more gray now
It's been a while since I've seen your picture
And sometimes your face eludes my memory
But maybe that's for the better
So I cross my fingers
      —And hope you've been gentle to the places
         where you've discovered the hurt

the bedpost + the conclusion

I trust the summer sun
    and the way I'm looked at these days
    by familiar eyes
    by passing gazes
words once so severely sought
    cottonwood cascading in July
    the value is mounting
    under the fitted sheets
        and oak tree shadows
        the era of reflective sighs
I used to take tallies of the time
    scratches in my bedpost
        blowing out candles
        wishing the cold away
    revisiting old haunts
        where I can see my handprints
        and watched the way horses moved
    I see longer hair and a short skirt
        but she has such a disfigured face
        what a natural pity
            knowing the ending now
            knowing the course of the *if*
           only

                    it's so hard to learn any
                    other way

it comes back around a time or two
        screenshots and receipts a reminder
                of steps in the sand
                of choices that don't make sense now
                tides once so cold to the touch
        nail-biting abandoned
                time unwasted when perspective is
                  gained
                my shoulders emblazoned with a price
                  seldom afforded
well wishes so fine
        a needle drops into the groove and its path is
          set
        I spin behind closed doors
                and laugh at the way my feet stumble
                because it's a secret I keep
        it's meaningless but it is not arbitrary
                this little mirth
                I see because I want to
                it clicks together with a snap
winning grins and honest confessions
        out of a crowd emerges my truest self
        with a stronger voice and weaker complicity
        eager with a yes when the time is right
                and grace with the grief and bitter
                  happenings

oh, growth, what a tricky thing
    laughter in hallways and bathroom
     compliments
    the spins a paramount regret
        just another case of the twenties
        such simple niceties and ironies and
        homilies
    passing remarks that I watch go by
        and wonder why it was such a hiccup
        to love and break this bread
            with taste meant to be sweet
            came out to be a little sour
maybe it was a trite dream
    to believe in the numbers
    the statistics of all the gods
        who I recognize in airport reflections
        who speak in tongues to bent ears
            and for a second maybe I
            almost drop it
            into a pool I thought infinite
            like galaxies
    was it delusion
        because I look at it through a crisp lens
        and wonder if hope has a second name

time zones are welcome divides
    clear and smokeless air
    I breathe clean when I see you
        a little space so unlike gravity

       even daylight can't expose the things
      so long gone
          because with the conclusion
             there is peace
once a tryst
now a bygone epoch
      I look to your face
         and I see what is past
         and I think no more

acknowledgments

Truly, it is so surreal to be writing something like an acknowledgements page. I recall the first year I started writing and receiving notebooks and pens for my birthday; since then I've held onto hope of one day seeing my work on a bookshelf. And there are so many people who have helped me get here whom I cannot imagine not thanking, including:

My husband, for believing in me from the very first time I read him a poem in the car, my voice and my hands shaking. My love, you are the greatest thing that I've ever had the privilege to call mine.

Claire, who spent many late nights with me on that emerald green couch and hashed it all out until there were no stones left to turn over. This collection would not have nearly as many layers if I did not have such a dear friend to bare my soul to.

Michael and the whole Orange Hat team, for taking a chance on me as a first time author and making this whole process so smooth. I am so honored and so proud to be one of the first Bubbler Press authors.

All my girls—who obviously kept their cool when I announced my book was getting published. Thank you for being my loudest, most enthusiastic cheerleaders.

And you! Yeah, you! Thank you for letting my work be a small part of your busy days, for taking the time to glimpse into the world of a woman trying to make sense of it all. It means more than you'll ever know.

www.ingramcontent.com/pod-product-compliance
Lightning Source LLC
LaVergne TN
LVHW010304070426
835507LV00033B/3498